MW00575836

HOMES *of* QUIET ELEGANCE

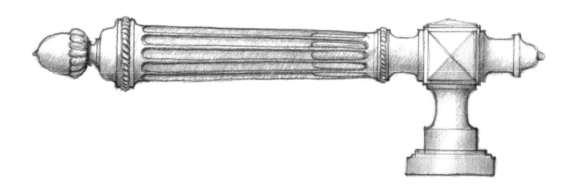

HOMES *of* QUIET ELEGANCE

A COLLECTION OF RECENT WORKS BY WADE WEISSMANN ARCHITECTURE

WADE WEISSMANN

WITH HENRIKA DYCK TAYLOR

Gibbs Smith

CONTENTS

INTRODUCTION   6

CALIFORNIA FARM RETREAT   8

NEW STRUCTURES FOR A STORIED ESTATE   34

BAY VILLA   50

LAKE MICHIGAN MODERN   80

PEACEFIELD FARM   94

GEORGIAN COUNTRY ESTATE   114

MIDWEST GREENHOUSE   150

MID-CENTURY REVIVAL   160

LAKE CLUB CABIN   178

GENEVA LAKE SPORTS BARN   204

LAKESIDE ESCAPE   220

DRAWING INSPIRATION   262

CREDITS   272

INTRODUCTION

From vegetables to jewelry, heirlooms have a story to tell. I love creating what we call "heirloom houses" because they are intended to last generations and carry traditions and memories forward even as new generations add their mark. I've been enthralled with this concept from a very young age and feel lucky that my profession allows for the manifestation of it.

When my team and I began to think about producing a second book as a follow-up to *Heirloom Houses: The Architecture of Wade Weissmann* (Gibbs Smith, 2018), I specifically imagined this new book you're holding to be approachable and conversational. I envisioned it to connect the dots between my personal ideas about design to our various outcomes and why that is attractive to our clients. Yes, many of our commissions are quite grand in scale and are intended to realize our clients' dreams of a lasting legacy. But at the core, I am interested in a zest and romance for life, honest materials and ingredients, utility, and functionality. These basic ingredients for living well were handed down to me by my family, instilling a nostalgia that's become almost a sixth sense for me. In other words, what endures has great appeal and nourishes my imagination. At the same time, life is ever-changing, and a part of the DNA of our firm involves embracing the dialogue about how architecture can adapt and be adapted during the course of a lifetime and for lifetimes to come.

When I was growing up, my parents bought forty acres of land near Lake Michigan, two hours away from Milwaukee. The existent farmhouse was reported to be haunted, so my mother refused to stay in it. Instead, three generations of us all slept in a migrant cottage in a grove of trees during the summers. We had no running water. It was a no-frills working farm life, and it was just wonderful. The microclimate there was ideal for growing currants, pears, and apples, so we produced delicious jams and my grandmother supervised everything about the process. We used black metal buckets hanging around our necks to collect the fruit. The haylofts were full of wooden ladders to use. We had a summer kitchen, and I can just see the hundreds and hundreds of jars of preserves filling the space. We worked hard, ate well, and slept deeply. We had a big open room upstairs with ten beds. It was a rustic, simple time that remains utterly romantic to me!

My experience on the family farm exemplifies a life where you were constantly challenged: managing a swarm of bees or caring for a sick animal demanded immediate response. Problem-solving while immersed in a specific task or environment is something I do all the time as an architect. These moments are the most rewarding assignments in my life. The byproduct of those challenging moments is the storytelling that comes out of it. For me, residential architecture is both the backdrop and a scrapbook for a life, so we conceive of dignified, delightful places that reflect the people who inhabit them, and the place gives value and quality to their experience. Residential architecture honors the individuals who live there, the authorship is impossible to establish, and the place endures for those reasons.

While in architecture school, I did my thesis on seasonal architecture like the place my family had. The memories of everyone sleeping in a hot attic and the sound of rain on the roof fueled my investigations about places that leave an indelible impression. Recalling a communal life where challenges and solutions belonged to us all remains palpable against a rustic backdrop of raw, durable materials. All that unfinished wood had warmth and it smelled good. Rough boards, all hand-hewn. It was real. Today, I believe I design—we design—to the kinds of memories and images that are incandescent for our clients, whatever they may be. Curling up in a dormer to read

during a thunderstorm; gathering around a lively, warm kitchen for a meal; cocktails on the porch overlooking a lake in the chill of the evening. We make it reality. It is interesting and timely to think about how the pandemic changed what home is to many of us. Despite the uncertainty and fear, it gave us a curious gift of time at home. Aspects of life at home took on a different hue and even urgency for our clients, and we were busier than ever.

At WWA, we engage ourselves deeply in every project entrusted to us and are keenly aware of the connections between them, but it is altogether different to actually articulate what they are and what our work means to our clients and to us. I hoped that by putting a thoughtful selection of material together this book would hone in on the stories and extraordinary people behind each project. I imagined we would see patterns emerge as stepping stones of insight into what we love to do and how we got here. For me, it is important that romance, utility, and durability mesh with the notion of "anonymous dignity," an idea that has stuck with me since graduate school, that architecture is most dignified and powerful when it cannot be attributed to a particular designer. I think this is exactly what we have demonstrated within these pages. I hope you will agree!

My grateful thanks to our loyal clients for all the exciting opportunities that stretch our creative limits. Thanks to my extraordinarily talented team for your dedication, passion, and continued pursuit of design excellence. Personal thanks to my friend and colleague of over twenty years, Eric Slavin, whose indelible design contributions can be seen and felt in many of the projects in this book. Our collaborations with designers, fabricators, landscape architects, contractors, and engineers heighten each experience and ground us in humility; together we continue to make the magic happen. Heartfelt thanks to Henrika Dyke Taylor, who helped me turn my personal memories and experiences into coherent sentences and to my family and loving partner for always supporting me and my ambitions.

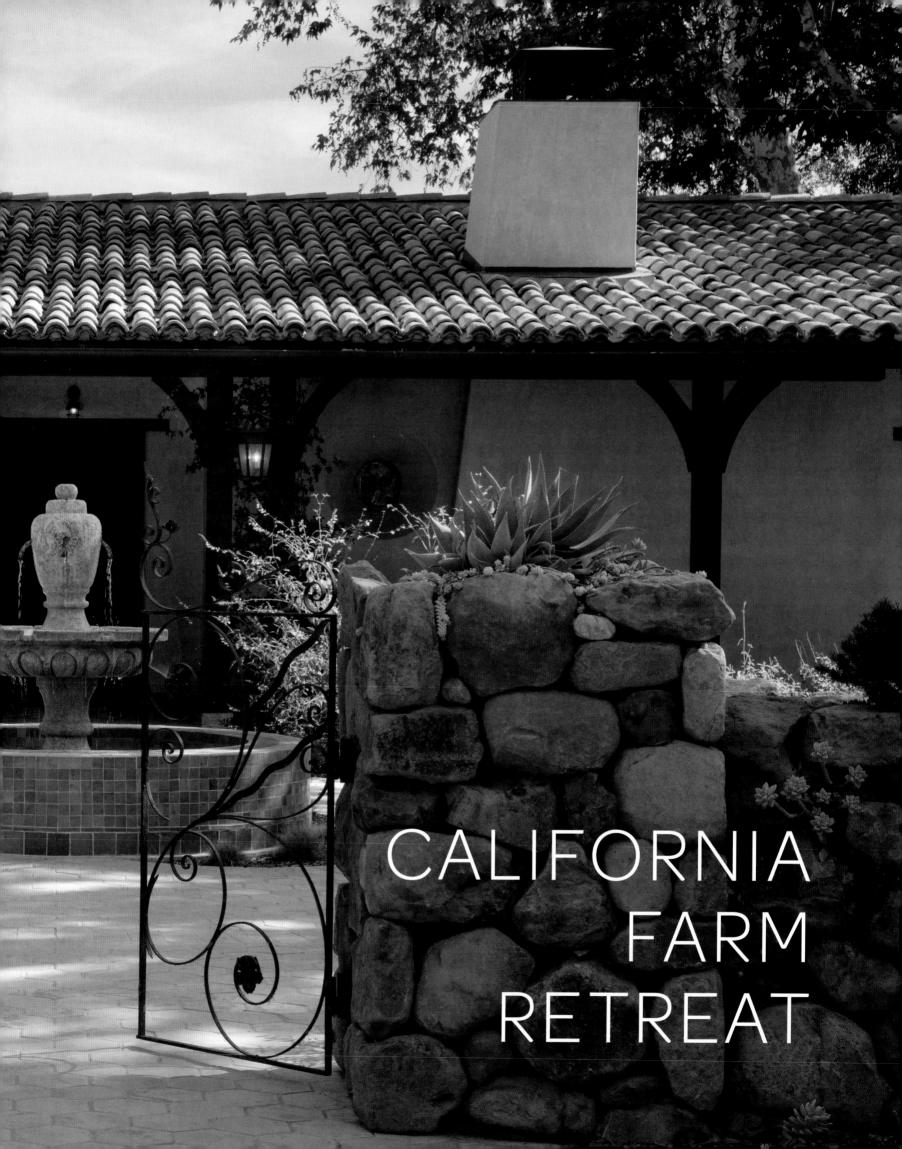

CALIFORNIA
FARM
RETREAT

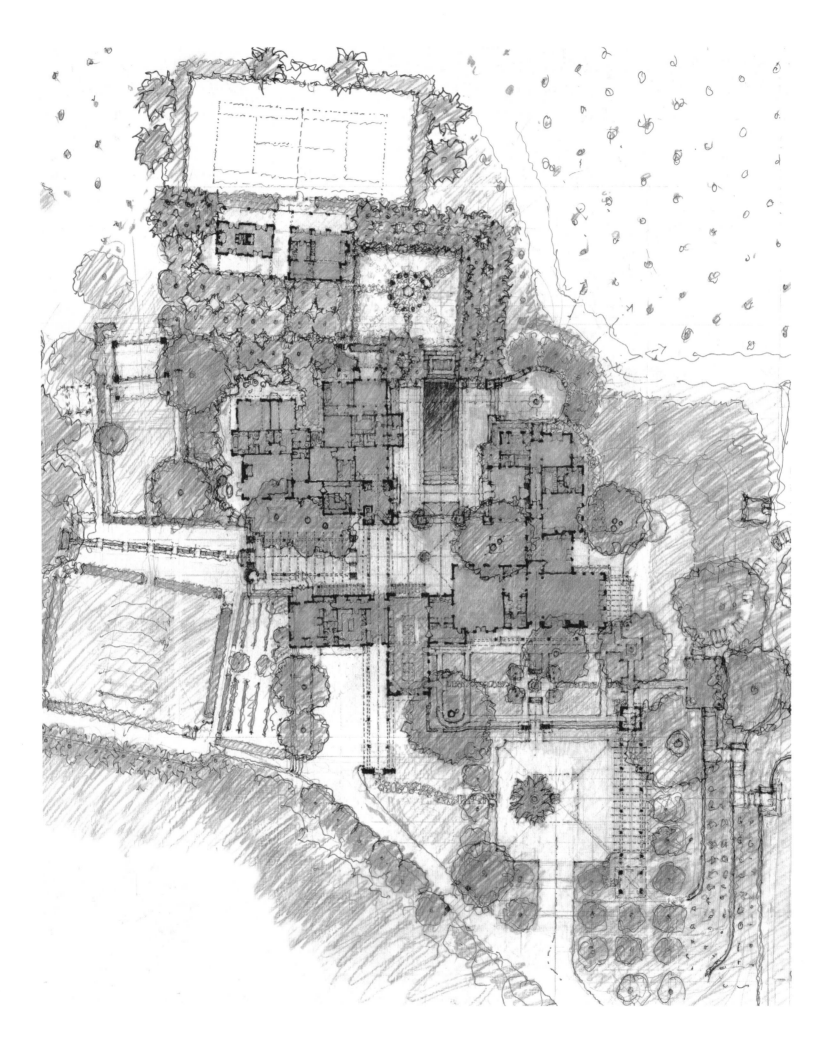

How we respond to our clients' deeply personal quests to create or improve a special place is the essence of our firm's portfolio—and this book. In this case, the new investor of a depleted lemon and avocado farm in Southern California brought an ambitious vision to the table. The overarching goal was to redefine the quality of what the farm produced with the intent that the farm would serve generations far into the future. We are always interested in contributing to a legacy to be handed down, so this project fired up our collective imaginations philosophically and architecturally.

We had designed a home previously for these clients, and that earlier relationship led us to become involved with the farm. There were several collaborators on this project who resonated with the effort and romance of family farming, the complexities of working a farm, and the resilience and creativity necessary to make it successful. It was an incredibly moving design experience for me to support the story and identity of this place. Our team worked in tandem with the Chicago-based interior designers Tina Simonds, Robert Alt, and Jordana Joseph, who contributed an eclectic collection of Americana to support the story and architectural forms.

The owners' plan included repurposing the existing structures on the site. Decades-old extensions on the property were mostly functional, and a large barn initially served as the headquarters for both the staff and visiting participants in an entrepreneurial farming program. The common interest in healthy living and foregoing the use of pesticides brought people together from across the country, but our clients wanted to go a step further to aesthetically unify the entire estate.

We devised a comprehensive site plan to be accomplished in phases, and an existing Spanish Colonial-style main house set the tone for architectural motifs and details. Annexed casitas provide accommodations for workers and visitors alike and create a residential compound where privacy, comfort, and community all coexist. A large, central gathering space draws people in for delicious, communal meals, while experimental kitchens, residential wings, courtyards, and a pool terrace were developed to beautiful yet practical effect.

This intricate project was six years in the making. Incredible patience, and a big dose of stereotypical Midwestern work ethic from all involved culminated in a unique enterprise centered on producing, preparing, and consuming incredible food. We had the opportunity to restructure and redefine a collage of agrarian forms. The focus of the design is utilitarian but exuberant, celebrating living outdoors and sheltering inside. Every component is responsive to the environment and the program for a farm with multiple destinations, which made the project interesting and exciting. It was a magical unfolding.

PAGES 8–9: Architectural cohesiveness throughout the farm complex is achieved with beautiful, natural materials. Stone, clay tile, wood, wrought iron, plaster, and stucco are accented with colorful tile and textiles. The entry courtyard gate with its delicate scroll and rose motif is from Architectural Artifacts in Chicago. The antique fountain is 17th-century Italian limestone from Ancient Surfaces in NYC, and the fountain basin's periwinkle tile is from Malibu Ceramic.

THIS SPREAD: View of the gardens and covered walkway from the arrival motor court. Sketch of outbuilding below.

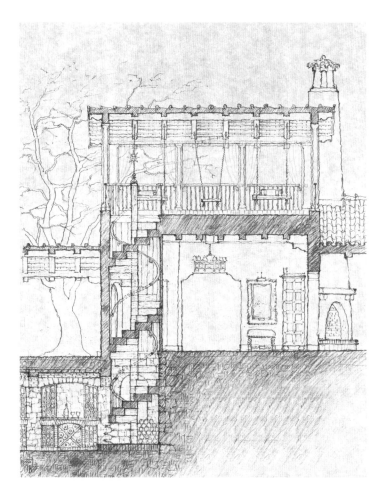

OPPOSITE TOP: An exotic and playful round daybed on wheels is suspended from the ceiling. The seamed, galvanized shade for the fixture above the daybed is from Big Daddy's Antiques.

OPPOSITE BOTTOM LEFT: Illustration of tower section.

OPPOSITE BOTTOM RIGHT: In the tower loft overlooking the pool, the delightful shape of the multicolored terra-cotta floor tile from Montana is called Moroccan Arabesque.

ABOVE: The pool court beckons with multicolored mosaic pool tile by Trend. An antique, amber lantern from Revival is suspended above the tower door on a new iron arm by Casa Del Sol Ironworks in Ventura.

ABOVE AND RIGHT: The outdoor dining pavilion brings everyone at the farm together under a canopy of twinkling orbs. The Spanish pierced ball lighting is by Revival Antiques in Pasadena.

OVERLEAF LEFT: A view of the workout pavilion front porch epitomizes the rustic sensibility and natural vegetation found throughout the farm.

OVERLEAF RIGHT: A cast-iron lion head from Architectural Artifacts in Chicago serves as the spigot for the pool cabana sink.

ABOVE: The Guesthouse great room dazzles with a Niermann Weeks art deco crystal chandelier hanging from a shimmering hand-stamped tin ceiling. The tall, almost delicate barn doors from Architectural Artifacts create a pleasing composition of forms and materials along with the restored pine cabinets and restored Carrara marble–topped table. The terra-cotta and marble flooring is new.

OPPOSITE: An antique icebox restored by Danlin Furniture Conservators in Chicago features its original handles, creating a kitchenette informed with functional, elegant simplicity. The copper sink and surround are vintage.

OPPOSITE AND ABOVE: Ambiguous as to whether they were new or restored, the interiors by Tina Simonds, Jordana Joseph, and Robert Alt achieve a rich, layered palette with natural materials and a sense of history and patina. From the entry space through the generous main gathering room, all the way to the large kitchen, the same plank wood flooring throughout grounds the exuberant variety of styles and furnishings.

BELOW: The large main kitchen carries the richness of material and form used throughout the farm complex. A skylight opens through the reclaimed beams of the ceiling, a restored and electrified chandelier hangs high, and mosaic tile enlivens the stove hood, which is supported by large wooden brackets. Herringbone overlay cabinetry for the refrigerators and wide plank floors make this kitchen (one of several) beautiful and efficient.

OPPOSITE: The Guesthouse kitchen has an eye-catching mint green cast-iron sink found in Oneonta, NY. The deep terra-cotta and black tiles are handmade, and the toolbox drawer handles are vintage. Wood-topped counters and a BlueStar stove complete this magical room.

PREVIOUS OVERLEAF: The test kitchen is the heartbeat of the farm. Terra Bardiglio tile covers the walls; the vent hood is custom, and the large white grill above it is reclaimed cast iron. The green drop pendants are from NY Lighting and the pot rack was made by Dennis Estrada of Casa del Sol. The vintage island was restored with a mitered drop in the marble top. The three-bowl sink is made from a stone slab, with a mitered drop in the marble top.

OPPOSITE: Old and new sinks and bath details. The tower powder room sink, top right, is new carved marble. The main house powder room sink, bottom right, is a 500-year-old Italian farmhouse sink.

ABOVE: A beamed bedroom features a nailhead headboard and a restored vintage glass light fixture. Antique doors slide to reveal a dresser repurposed as the bathroom vanity.

ABOVE: Hearkening back to an earlier era with a speakeasy sensibility, the reclaimed Chicago brick wall and ceiling tiles warm the farm's wine cellar, which holds up to 3,000 bottles of wine.

OPPOSITE: Arched cellar doors are by Steelworks. The whiskey lounge wraps its patrons in a warm embrace with leather-tiled flooring and wool fabric–paneled wall. The corner cascading light fixture is custom made. Back bar vintage light with crystal beading is from Remains. Asymmetrical bar (front) features Scandinavian burnished gold stools.

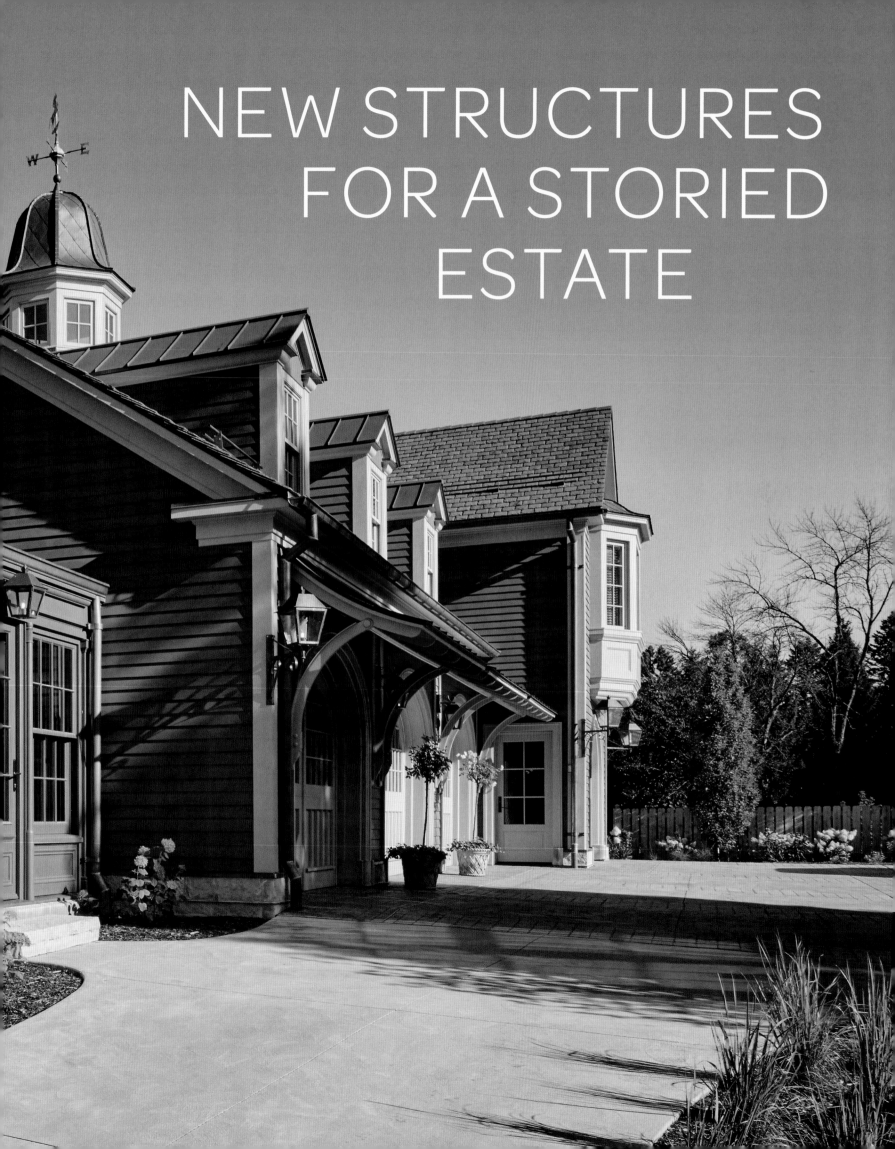

NEW STRUCTURES FOR A STORIED ESTATE

The commission for a special building to showcase the clients' collection of automobiles led to the design and construction of not just the collector's barn, which is complementary to the Georgian manor style of the existing stone residence, but also of the service area for the entire estate. Subsequently, a pool pavilion was added to complete the array of smaller jewel box-like buildings created by our team for this special landscape.

The genesis for these opportunities came nearly thirty years prior via my older cousin, interior designer Jon Schlagenhaft (1958–2008), who had been a mentor to me. The property owners had engaged Jon in the late 1980s after purchasing the extant 1920s estate home and surrounding twenty acres, and Jon introduced me to the project while I was still in graduate school. My first impression of this particular house and the clients' lifestyle stuck with me. The experience, and ensuing relationship, was the seed that convinced me to dedicate my career to residential architecture for clients like these who desired a home that would endure, uphold family traditions, and delight for generations to come.

The example set by these clients and Jon's design acumen set the path and a standard that our firm has followed ever since, but the chance to work with this family did not come until several decades later. As a collector of vintage and custom cars, the husband housed his automobiles in assorted structures on the property, all the while envisioning an architecturally distinguished, commodious garage more in keeping with the style of the main house. After meeting on the property, I proposed an elevated collector's garage that would not only display the collection but would provide space to entertain fellow auto enthusiasts and guests. The service areas for the estate were also redesigned around a romantic concept of English estate service buildings—lovely destinations set into the landscape that serve a utilitarian purpose. In tandem with many design professionals, including Wirtz International (Arthur Ross Award winner 2023), who created the recent updates to the landscape and gardens for this property, our team aimed to beautifully incorporate the land and the architecture into a unified scheme.

The light-filled garage features a steel structure, polished flooring, and custom windows and doors. Copper gutters, seamed copper overhangs, a cupola, and a stone base reinforce the notion that this detail-rich garage was always part of the estate. In addition to the car bays, a greenhouse for winterizing the property's gardenia trees was added to the program, and a well-appointed apartment above offers a chic venue for small cocktail parties. The large basement, with concrete plank floors, serves both as the auto mechanic shop and maintenance workshop for the estate.

During the process of creating the garage, the client mentioned he'd always dreamed of a pool house. A glamorous, flat-roofed structure clad in painted white brick was the result and is intentionally very different from the garage. Channeling the classic movie *The Philadelphia Story*, with the contrast of sleek pool house next to the stately Main Line mansion, we brought that vision to bear here. The elegant geometry of the existing pool is surrounded by a stone terrace with a spectacular view of the grounds. In turn, the terrace is rimmed by hedges with forestation beyond. The pool house complex, with its Lutyens-esque detailing, includes a spa at the opposite end and a firepit on the side. The pavilion's front façade opens completely to a layered vista of pool, firepit, spa, terrace, and side elevation of the house via twelve-foot-high bronze-and-steel doors on a concave track inspired by the pool's curved shape. Inside, brick-sized limestone pavers match those of the main residence porch, and the broad fireplace with symmetrical inglenooks beckons. You can almost imagine Tracy Lord (played by Katherine Hepburn) taking a nap here after an invigorating swim or having cocktails around the firepit on a perfect summer evening.

For all of us, it was a keenly felt privilege to work with these clients who are respected patrons of their city. They love life, live large, and desired beautiful places to gather and entertain in keeping with family traditions and an established lifestyle. The new structures gleam with extraordinary design details and craftsmanship, all while making the setting of a storied estate complete.

LEFT: The reclaimed hexagonal terra-cotta tile floor of the greenhouse is a pleasing and practical detail. Fabricated in the UK by Westbury Conservatories, the room was assembled on-site for the purpose of winterizing the property's gardenia trees.

OPPOSITE: Tile on the wainscot and cove detail wraps the walls around the primary automobile display space. The pitched ceiling is supported by blackened steel trusses and features butt-jointed, whitewashed, wide plank cedar. The floor is polished concrete with exposed aggregate.

ABOVE: The powder room glistens with antiqued limestone wet walls and a high-gloss lacquer paint influenced by Hermès classic orange.

RIGHT: The upper-level entertaining area has a painted, butt-jointed wood plank ceiling with profiled battens. Interior details such as the geometric cowhide area rug, pewter fireplace mantel, and LED-integrated chandelier create a cozy atmosphere, punctuated by the convenience of a kitchen.

ABOVE: The well-appointed guest suite with a balcony overlooking the grounds boosts a custom upholstered bed frame and decorative ceiling fixture.

OPPOSITE: Honed black granite countertops, porcelain textured wall tile, nickel sink faucets by Waterworks, and painted cabinetry with built-in vanity mirrors grace the elegant bathroom.

PRECEDING OVERLEAF: The flat-roofed pool pavilion features bronze and steel doors on a concave track inspired by the pool's geometry. The exterior façade is painted brick, with inset custom blackened metal trellises surrounding the windows. Copper caps and lamb's tongue scuppers add dimension and glam to the Lutyens-esque detailing.

OPPOSITE & ABOVE: Inside, the floor is comprised of reclaimed brick pavers and cream limestone cut in a large diamond pattern. The ceiling is pecky cypress infilled with painted wood trim. Walls of Venetian plaster and antique furnishings add a Moroccan flair to the living space.

BAY VILLA

Miami is the dynamic setting for this reimagined home. The clients are contemporary art afficionados who thought they found the perfect house for their collection and lifestyle. The home was well designed and built by architect Z. W. Jarosz; it features high ceilings to accommodate large works, and has a gorgeous view across Biscayne Bay. The couple brought in Mark Weaver & Associates as their interior designers to create a glamorous art deco-inspired interior; however, Mark quickly identified key elements that the house was lacking based on his intimate understanding of the clients' lifestyle after working together for decades. Built in the early 2000s, the house had visual appeal, but the interior circulation and refinement of detail and light would require updates to meet our clients' needs. What began as a suggestion to move a wall and add a sitting room, ultimately, developed into a stunning design transformation of the interior of the house and landscape.

As of this writing, our firm is currently creating architecture for the clients in other locations—Los Angeles and Montecito—so our ongoing relationship brings a level of familiarity and trust. For this Miami residence, we envisioned a tropical version of an urbane New York City townhouse. To resolve some design objectives without altering the footprint or exterior façade, we enlarged or added windows and reorganized the vertical circulation of the house by significantly altering the entry and stair halls. The resulting reclaimed space allows for internal connectiveness, flow, and opportunities to bring in natural light. The second floor was reconfigured completely to accommodate a primary bedroom suite with a new adjoining outdoor terrace. A gym was added, and all the public spaces became more defined.

Interior gestures like the wave motif of the entry stair railing, the living room cornice, and the re-design of the living room fireplace with flanking arched etageres reinforce the refined interior. In the living room we created a new pillowed ceiling with custom plaster cornice molding, achieving an elegant outcome where all components adhere to the scale of the room.

Once the interior architecture and scale was right, we had the framework to showcase a sublime level of detail—the fantastic lighting, inside and out, by Nathan Orsman's firm, the steel and glass doors, beautiful wall coverings, and a sophisticated bar. The clients' art collection encompasses a broad array of large, significant pieces, objet d'art, table settings, and glassware. Everything is beautifully displayed and at home.

Outside, the surrounding garden and existing pool were re-envisioned for optimal exterior space. A terrace, the pool, and a gazebo by the water complete the waterfront landscape. At the entry, we refined the arrival sequence, which includes a long fountain allée and a new motor court and walkway.

Sometimes as architects we get to design from scratch, but here, a luminous new version of this house came about from significantly rearranging the walls, a feat that required a high level of project management and deft interior design. It demonstrates what is possible when you go the distance. The entirety of our intervention epitomizes how the clients live and entertain. All that they wanted from their house was realized.

PAGES 52–53: To fill this home with coastal light, we enlarged or added new windows at several elevations.

OPPOSITE: In the entry forecourt fountain pool, seen here through the front door with reimagined plaster cornices, a bronze sculpture by Maillol adds a serene focal point to the composition. Inside the foyer hangs a spectacular painting from the clients' collection by Joan Mitchell.

BELOW: The gracious entry hall displays a large pink acrylic sculpture by DeWain Valentine. The original stair hall was opened here with an expansive, segmented arch to bring additional natural light into the entry. A custom wave-inspired baluster and added stair hall paneling complete the transformation.

LEFT: Architectural detail in the millwork and the single coffer between the seating area and the bar define the comfortable family room. An arched screen opens to the breakfast nook and bar. Two art deco–style recliners designed by Rose Tarlow are inviting in orange; the fabric is by Rubelli. The gilt bronze and parchment coffee table is ample for drinks, snacks, and reading material. The painting is by George Condo.

ABOVE: Arched floor-to-ceiling French doors look out into the garden from behind light and airy curtains beckoning to the outdoors.

OVERLEAF LEFT: The lacquer and bronze design of the bar was inspired by Miami's famed Surf Club. Mirrored doors, custom painted in verre églomisé, by MJ Atelier artfully camouflage the bar storage above the bronze-accented, ivory-fluted front. The bar top is made of onyx. Barstools are by Dylan Farrell.

OVERLEAF RIGHT: In keeping with the bayside milieu, an under the sea–inspired breakfast nook carries the theme with a unique coral and crystal seashell chandelier by Fisher Weisman. The eucalyptus wood table by Rossi Antiques pivots to accommodate seating for five to eight.

PRECEDING OVERLEAF: The ethereal dining room presents a myriad of custom elements. The bas-relief dimensional wall covering in a foliage pattern is by MJ Atelier in Los Angeles. A new plaster cornice, cove lighting, and a jib door for discreet service entry were added here. An evocative sea-creature-like chandelier, the art deco fabric by Prelle, NY, Buccellati silver, and Koman-inspired servers crafted in walnut and glass contribute to the magical space, which shimmers here in the early dusk light.

RIGHT: The sophisticated, cheerful living room overlooks the pool and bay. It's style reflects the dialogue between the client, interior designer, and architect. The color scheme and art deco chairs are inspired by 1930s Miami. Illuminated niches and wave motif moldings help compose the space for select artwork: a Jean-Michel Basquiat painting hangs above the fireplace and the sculptures are by Parpin.

PRECEDING OVERLEAF RIGHT: The main-floor guest bedroom is transformed into a light-filled haven that opens to the garden. The circa-1960s ceiling light fixture adds a modern flair to the classically paneled space. Bespoke linens are by Sfera.

ABOVE & OPPOSITE: The luxe primary bath is completely new and includes custom fluted Hollywood-deco vanities with onyx countertops. The tub is customized with fluted millwork to match. The mural by MJ Atelier sets the tropical scene, while the vintage Lalique chandelier offers 1920s glamour. The plumbing fixtures and decorative pulls are by P. E. Guerin. Flooring is by Artistic Tile in Onyx and Thassos marble in Lily Pad design. Bon Vivant created the bronze framing around the mirrors, window, and tub niche. The rock crystal shell sconces are by Paul Ferrante.

ABOVE: Prelle-designed fabric and Samuel and Sons trim adorn this daybed by Pollaro. The throw is by Loro Piana.

RIGHT: The dressing room for him is a study in custom walnut cabinetry. Handsomely detailed throughout, the island top is inlaid with cognac-colored alligator. The pendants, circa 1960, are by Mazzega. Satin nickel olive knuckle hinges by Lowe Hardware; stepped cabinet pulls by Sherle Wagner.

OVERLEAF: In her dressing room, the multicolored, hand-blown Murano glass ceiling fixture is "The Bouquet" by John Salibello. Her island top is inlaid with rose-patterned stamped leather. The fluting motif is evident in the custom millwork and the accent mirror panels. The bench cushion is upholstered in custom fabric by Fortuny.

LEFT: Fresh and light, the primary bedroom and sitting room have new plaster cornices, a pillowed ceiling, and fluted coffer plaster detail. French doors open to a new balcony overlooking the pool terrace and bay. Above the seating area is a Paul Ferrante crystal palm-leaf chandelier; the side table in rosewood and shagreen is by Ruhlmann.

ABOVE: The chaise is matched with a side table by Paula Swinnen, an artist from Belgium.

ABOVE LEFT: A powder room features a custom sink console, wall covering in silk ecru, and sconces from Pierre Frey.

ABOVE RIGHT: The interior architecture and millwork create a pleasing order at the top of the stairs, where a window was added to again capitalize on the Sunshine State's promise.

OPPOSITE: A new stone patio overlooking the pool terrace and bay offers an intimate seating area perfect for morning coffee or conversation.

OPPOSITE: The lighted forecourt fountain at dusk makes a statement on arrival.

ABOVE: The infinity pool, pool house, and garden terrace newly engage with the house and views of the bay. The new pool is edged with Dominican keystone and merges into the completely redesigned landscape.

OPPOSITE: View of the infinity pool with a dramatic evening sky over the bay. A new glass seawall virtually disappears, enhancing the views of the spectacular sunsets.

ABOVE: Perfect for entertaining or solitary enjoyment, the pool house and terrace are beautifully lighted whatever the occasion.

LAKE MICHIGAN
MODERN

PRECEDING OVERLEAF: The exterior view of the front façade shows the gabled roof of the garage punctuated by shed dormers. Clad windows and cedar lintels are set into the bluestone entry porch and the façade of spit face, rock face, and bed face stone.

OVERLEAF: A monochromatic palette of white board and batten, black clad windows, and a blend of gray and natural stone complements the light and shadow of the details.

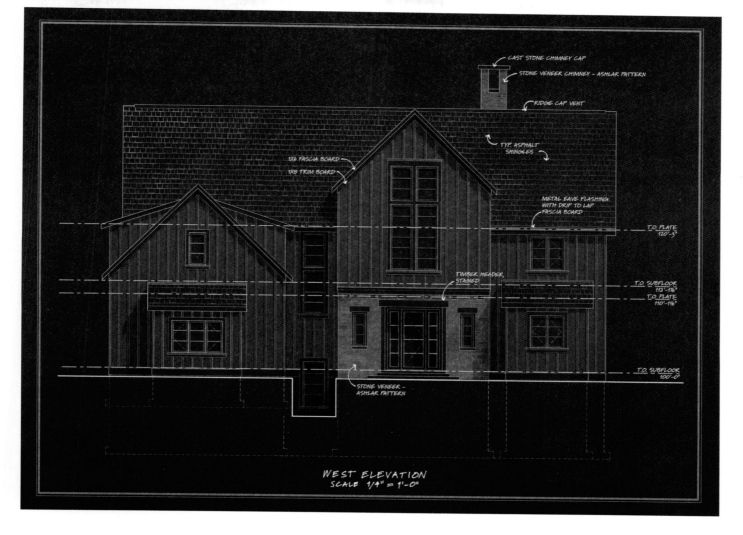

WEST ELEVATION
SCALE 1/4" = 1'-0"

A narrow lot with sublime views of Lake Michigan captured the imagination of our clients. They wanted a new primary residence for their growing family and came to us for the design. The property, located in a northern suburb of Milwaukee, rises sixty feet up from the water's edge all the way to a bluff, presenting a dramatic slice of land with a tight buildable area. For a tale of "form follows circumstances," as our studio director Tom Wynn likes to say, the topography at the top of bluff and solar orientation determined the siting and shape of the house. A zoning variance permitted us to position the house closer to the street, which allowed for space at the rear for a terrace and lawn.

On arrival, a three-bay garage and generous entry court sets the tone along with a tall casement window showcasing the sculptural stair within. The lake is visible through the house, and views are framed from nearly every room. To the rear, a patio is defined by a low, curved stone wall and comfortable seating around a firepit. Maximizing the views and the axial relationships through the house were touchstones to the plan. Everything else fell under the editing process, rendering the design and the clients' program down to what is essential: proportion and connectivity.

At first blush, the home is transitional, or downright contemporary, which is a departure for our firm. Generally, our focus is on traditional and vernacular design, and indeed, while this project is streamlined and assembled to function well, the exterior board and batten siding and natural stone in an ashlar pattern offer simplicity and familiarity. As our clientele becomes younger and wants our expertise and experience to inform something different, we get to be nimble about how we work. Every commission is a vote of confidence and an opportunity to stretch our abilities. When owners want to work with us, we forge ahead to create their version of a heritage home, not ours. This light-filled residence is very much in that spirit.

PRECEDING OVERLEAF LEFT: The solid white oak treads of the custom metal stair match the white oak hardwood flooring used throughout the house.

PRECEDING OVERLEAF RIGHT: Dramatic contrast in the kitchen comes from the blackened steel range and integrated cabinetry against a full-height stone backsplash and a waterfall island countertop.

OPPOSITE: The four-season room has a stone fireplace for chilly days and evenings and views to the lake on three sides.

ABOVE: The lower-level recreation space with wet bar, billiards room, and gym delivers on drama with a moody palette and industrial vibe.

OVERLEAF LEFT & RIGHT: A blackened steel fireplace surround with exposed rivets creates a bold effect against the restrained plaster detailing in the living area. Finished to match the white oak ceiling beams, jambs frame generous views to the lake.

PEACEFIELD
FARM

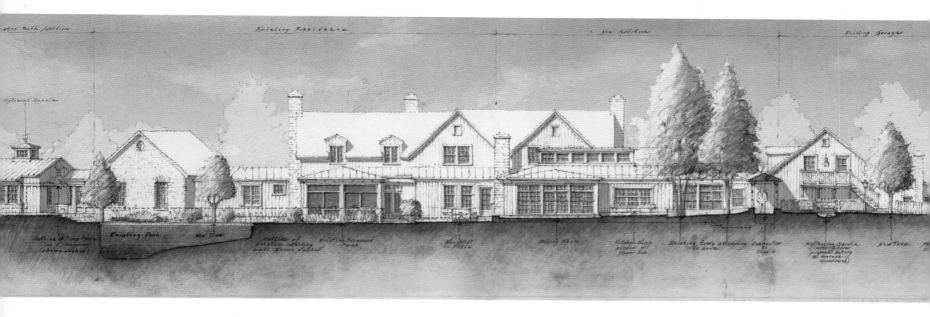

This gorgeous farm property had a pre-Civil War cabin on it, a detached garage, a large barn, and other ancillary buildings when our clients bought it. They were completely enamored with the scenery and tranquility of the place. Our assignment was to make all the pieces make sense as a whole, retain a sense of simplicity and calm, and accommodate family life and entertaining. The result is this wonderful ramble of charming vernacular architecture.

We all felt that we were part of a special relationship over the course of the project. The enthusiasm and exchange of ideas led our team and the clients to the point of finishing each other's sentences. Our connection has definitely developed into a long-term relationship, and we shared a huge amount of creative energy, collaborative power, and inspirational give and take.

We began by connecting the old cabin, which became the dining room, to the garage with a covered connector and mud hall. The front porch of the cabin remains the main entrance for visitors, accessible by a red brick walkway. Another brick walkway leads both up a few stairs to the mud hall or past the garage, with its standing seam copper overhang, to the rear dining terrace with outdoor fireplace. We added a bright, airy kitchen with clerestory windows where the visible chinking mortar inside is a nod to the origins of the house. Ultimately, when the owners were expecting their third child, we added a second story and a primary suite with his and hers dressing areas.

While the master plan provided infrastructure and useful components like the mud hall, a work-room, and a home office, we had to be thoughtful about fitting in additional programing as the house evolved. We loved that it was important to the owner to recycle existing building materials and match the farmhouse character in every element. We delighted in the finishes, how there are multiple ways to access the outdoors, and how the spaces are grouped. Our contractor was an important part of the process, and he continues to work on the house. Derrick Dennis was the project manager, and he was completely aligned with us to coauthor the project.

Inside and out, this homestead exudes charm and warmth. Friends and family visit often, driving past the bucolic landscape up the pebble driveway to the new entrance court. The owners love this place. They inspired the outcome.

LEFT: This view from the motor court shows the original cabin now extended via a connector to the garage. This and other additions enlarge and modernize the home while retaining the scale and character.

ABOVE: The connector is comprised of three parts: the enclosed mud hall that leads into the kitchen; the open, covered walkway; and the covered seating area on the side of the garage.

OPPOSITE TOP: The rendering shows the concept of the charming connector that makes the house and garage contiguous while also creating space for the mud hall and the covered outdoor walkway.

OPPOSITE BOTTOM: The original front porch of the existing cabin is the main entrance to the house for guests, who step through time into a rustic space reconceived as the main dining room.

ABOVE: The primary suite addition has a private side porch and pergola for the homeowners to enjoy.

PRECEDING OVERLEAF LEFT AND RIGHT: This wardrobe room and bath are part of the primary suite and features custom millwork and cabinetry. The sketch shows the built-in bench at the bay window.

LEFT: The new kitchen addition slopes off the back of the original cabin, which is now the dining room. Clerestory windows, Taj Mahal Quartzite countertops, and milk paint on the brick compose a bright, fresh, inviting space.

ABOVE: The existing chinked wall of the cabin provides texture and context in the new kitchen, designed for gathering family and friends.

OVERLEAF LEFT: The bright new mud hall has plenty of storage and hooks for kids and adults to hang their coats and drop off their bags.

OVERLEAF RIGHT: Whether utilized for fun or function, the farmhouse offers getaway spaces for study, creativity, and the simple tasks of daily living. The informal music room features a full bath and wet bar.

LEFT AND ABOVE: In her pretty bathroom, which looks out to the pool terrace, honed Carrara tile wainscot and countertops gleam in contrast to the painted millwork. The pale blue painted ceiling and louvered doors give a porch-like sensibility to the room.

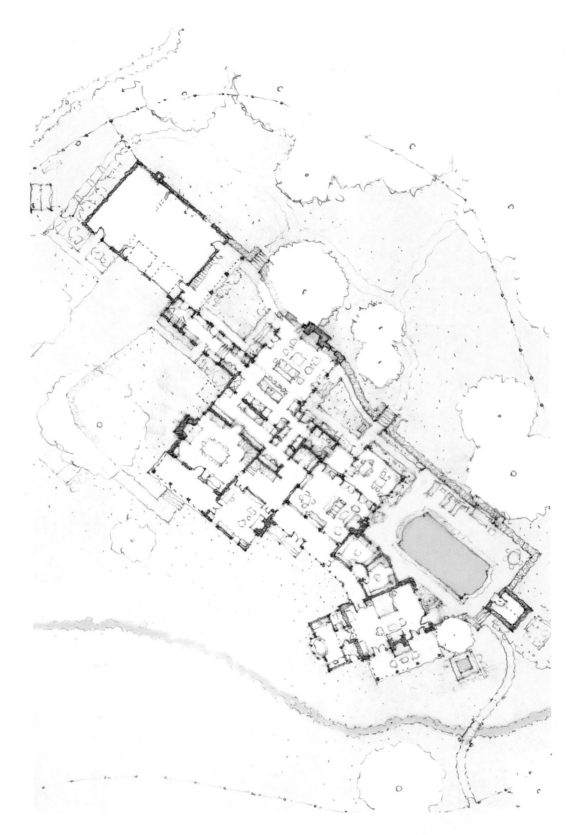

OPPOSITE TOP: Several outdoor rooms offer a variety of spaces for entertaining or private contemplation. The bricked kitchen terrace is comfortably bounded by the covered porch of the garage, the large stone fireplace and wall, and the screened-in porch.

OPPOSITE BOTTOM: The pool terrace completes the linear outdoor space on the other side of the screened-in porch. The woodland setting lies just beyond the stone retaining wall and back fencing.

ABOVE: The site plan shows how the house extends and is settled into the landscape.

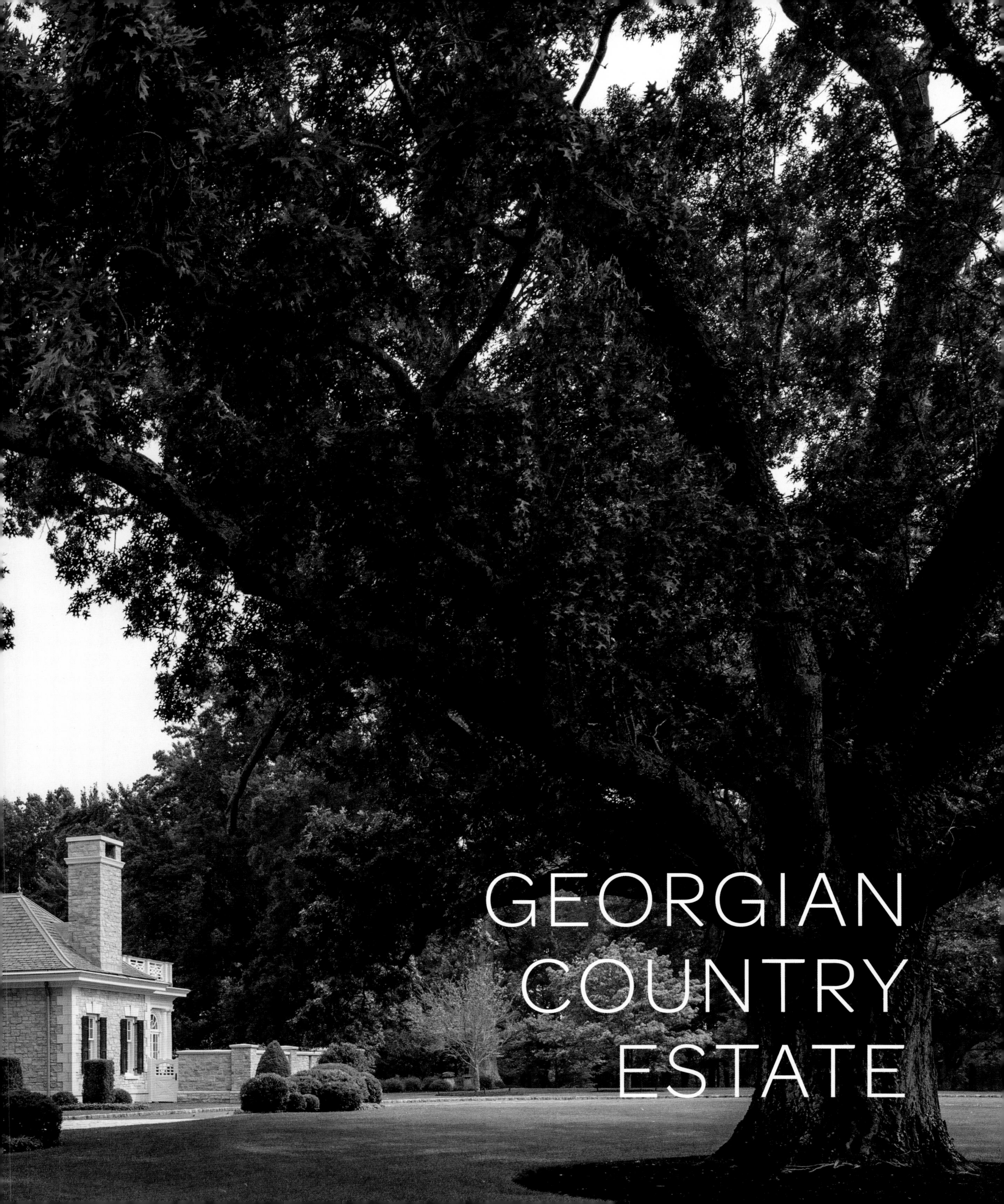

GEORGIAN
COUNTRY
ESTATE

The design objective for this extraordinary project was to create a grand country estate from which the clients could conduct their storied philanthropic entertaining, host friends and family, and still have quiet, intimate spaces to enjoy themselves. For this commission of a lifetime, our design team partnered with the clients, who were active from the beginning, Bunny Williams of Williams Lawrence for the interior design and decoration, and Ben Page of Page Landscape.

The project was driven by a high level of expectation and a collective desire to carefully balance the technical and functional requirements of the project without sacrificing aesthetics. To that end, the clients had the utmost regard for Bunny Williams and her team. Their methods and dedication elevated the entire process and made the experience memorable for everyone. While Bunny collaborated on the interior architecture, our studio director Tom Wynn managed the massive project with rigor and passion.

Architecturally, traditions established by both English and American Georgian country houses set the design precedent. Inspired by the site, the centerpiece of which features a grove of several-hundred-year-old oak trees, the owners desired their new home to evoke the presence of a stately historic residence. Thus, a classic Georgian style with chiseled stone and ornate door surrounds met the requirements of a family with their own deep heritage. The master plan of the fifty-acre property encompasses the monumental main house, brick drive, garage with cupola, maintenance buildings, pool house, greenhouse, garden, and lakeside Teahouse folly.

After first walking the site in 2013, I sketched a plan with what I thought was essential to the property. Captivated, the clients dove right in as our team maintained careful study to ensure the exterior character and embellishments were historically accurate and elegantly composed. The resulting stone house with limestone quoins features a grand entry with stairway, an enfilade of rooms along the rear elevation, and Palladian windows looking out to the bucolic surroundings and man-made lake. The opulent interior plan is defined by beautifully scaled and appointed rooms and the highest level of bespoke utility. From storing and displaying an extensive collection of china and glassware to how the wardrobes are organized, these details are as integral as the spaces dedicated to family enjoyment and privacy that make such a big house feel intimate.

Entertaining is a huge part of the program as well as accommodating a large staff and the clients' collections. The infrastructure, planning, and expectation for the house and property are equivalent to a five-star hotel combined with a civil works project. Meal preparation for intimate family dinners, or for gatherings of up to 800 people, required meticulous kitchen planning and design, while stormwater management systems were integrated into the entertainment lawn. Every conceivable detail was considered for function and beauty inside and out.

In particular, providing discreet circulation of staff was paramount in order to run the household smoothly. Our designers interviewed the house managers and staff about their jobs, and plans were drawn to their specifications and requirements. A staff entrance, rooms for rest and meals, and access corridors and entryways ensure that service is flawless and invisible.

Four years in the making, the main house, entry court, and service yard are carefully situated between the three largest and oldest oak trees, as if they had grown up around the house. The dramatic approach by Ben Page winds through the woods and past a serene field of prairie grasses and wildflowers before arriving at the motor court. A separate service road enters the garage courtyard between a pair of whimsical utility pavilions. On axis with the front door of the house, the lake is graced with a small, classically proportioned Teahouse. Completed in 2018, the house provided a refuge for the extended family during the COVID-19 pandemic shutdown.

It is impossible for us to talk about the success of this project without talking about Bunny. It was a huge team effort, and it was important to the client to work with someone with such a design pedigree. Bunny and her team were collaborative, generous, and indefatigable. Their expertise goes beyond the 'ordinary' tasks of personally supervising the selection and placement of the furnishings, wall coverings, and window treatments, but extends as a pragmatic understanding of the owners' lifestyle. They displayed a sensitivity to practicality and function without sacrificing aesthetics, which was astonishing to witness. Everyone put their heart and soul into this commission.

OPPOSITE TOP: A view through the motor court and porte cochere to the entry court beyond is framed between two utility pavilions.

OVERLEAF: A bedroom looks to the south-facing walled garden, a colorful, private sanctuary. In this view, the Teahouse folly is visible across the lake. Zinc-coated copper and slate roof terraces with Chippendale railings provide optimal viewing to the front and rear of the property.

OPPOSITE: Detail of entablature with triglyph and modillions.

ABOVE: The picturesque Teahouse is a nod to traditional Georgian "temple style" follies placed as a focal point to draw one's eye into the landscape.

OVERLEAF LEFT: The center hall opens to the living and dining rooms and is on axis with the Teahouse across the lake.

OVERLEAF RIGHT: Delicate de Gournay paper wraps the top portion of the stair hall, while corresponding hand-painted murals are set in the lower panels.

PRECEDING OVERLEAF LEFT: A grand overdoor in the entry features a hand-carved acorn finial crowning an arched broken pediment.

PRECEDING OVERLEAF RIGHT: Charles Edwards lanterns grace the primary bedroom gallery.

ABOVE: The scroll of the bracketed tread is a subtle embellishment in keeping with the slender elegance of the stair spindles.

RIGHT: A carved limestone fireplace surround takes place of honor in the bright gathering room.

The walnut sitting room has a delicate gold leaf Greek key in the cornice and a radial pattern in the arched window transoms of the doors. An integrated jib door leads to the primary suite.

ABOVE: A gold-leaf mirror surround with broken pediment conceals a television behind it.

OPPOSITE: A custom bronze door by Historical Arts & Casting leads to the wine room. The adjacent bar/butler's pantry features brass accents and pewter countertops.

ABOVE: The Palladian window in the study is paneled in walnut. The surround conceals solar shades integrated into the assembly.

OPPOSITE: In the study, the walls are upholstered. The desk is flanked by antique globes and portraits of Abraham Lincoln. An ornate, Federal-style chandelier hangs from the plaster tracery ceiling.

OVERLEAF: The formal dining room features a dentilated cornice with egg-and-dart molding. A Murano glass chandelier, Jamb marble mantel, Gracie Studio wall covering, and mirrored screen provide a feast for the senses.

ABOVE: Butler's pantry with service stair features a mirrored backsplash and pewter countertops..

OPPOSITE: In the primary kitchen, decorative china adorns the wall over the Palladian window.

RIGHT: The delightful breakfast room, with treillage by Accents of France, is a sophisticated garden room with panoramic views of the landscape.

OVERLEAF LEFT: A walnut-paneled gentleman's dressing room features a gold-leaf Greek key motif with view into his bath.

OVERLEAF RIGHT: Her primary bath. The mirror and radial muntin over the vanity echo the exterior window composition.

PAGE 144: The side entry hall mural was relocated from the owners' previous dining room.

PAGE 145: A barrel-vaulted lobby hall leads to formal ladies' and gentlemen's powder rooms.

ABOVE: The treillage panels of the pool house look beyond to the treillage breakfast room in the distance, creating a visual continuity of detail and ornament.

OPPOSITE: From across the lake, the Teahouse has a commanding view of the rear elevation, which is framed by two heritage oak trees.

MIDWEST
GREENHOUSE

The challenge of merging utility with aesthetically pleasing design creates an opportunity for creativity, and our team was energized by this chance to seamlessly situate a new glasshouse to the existing Tudor home of our client. An avid horticulturalist, she gave us a clear objective to build a highly functioning greenhouse to replace potting sheds that did not add architectural cohesion to her property. The timber, stone, and brick Tudor style of the existing 1920s house inspired our design and use of materials for an integrated master plan. We were able to match the original local fieldstone to wrap the base of a new covered connector and the greenhouse. The same stone is used for the parapet walls that bookend the greenhouse. The low retaining walls that define the front terrace also utilize the buff-colored Wisconsin stone. A limestone cap further unifies the entire complex.

Our team worked in close collaboration with landscapers Scott Byron & Co. to ensure the landscape and architecture were in concert, merging new construction with the existing residence and property. Exuberant flower gardens at the front elevation recall a charming English garden, while geometric parterres at the back offer a quiet orderliness bordered by pavers.

Hartley Botanic, the venerable UK manufacturer, created the custom greenhouse, which was made to order based on the client's requirements and our specifications. In addition to its visual appeal, the greenhouse has a mechanical ventilation system, big potting tables, and sinks. Cold frames for starting plants from seed and hardening are set just outside. The arcade with its sundeck on top integrates the greenhouse structure logically to the house and simultaneously creates space for the dining and entertaining terrace at the front elevation.

The combination of an enthusiastic client, a talented team of artisans, and excellent masons brought all the components together. The stonework throughout extends the character of the house, and that's a testament to the dedication of the craftsmen, who were as passionate about their contributions as the designers. The side parapet of the greenhouse features a Dutch door and precision cut voussoir blocks to grace the arch. English Tudor brackets, lanterns, and copper flashing complete the vision here.

PAGE 152: The parapet end wall features an arched opening with voussoir stone and terra-cotta brick inlays. The limestone veneer and style correspond with the existing Tudor residence.

PAGES 154–55: A connector breezeway with roof terrace joins the new greenhouse to the main residence via the chef's kitchen on the main level and bedroom on the second level, for convenient access to the herb garden and a sitting porch, respectively.

PAGES 156–57: A view of the south-facing dining terrace, the breezeway connector, and the bespoke Hartley Botanic Victorian glasshouse with its dark brown finish.

ABOVE: A watercolor rendering depicts the greenhouse and connector seamlessly integrated into the existing Tudor-style residence nestled within the landscape.

BELOW: In the evenings, the glasshouse comes alive with illumination, while just around the corner you can spy a new north-facing terrace, and parterre flower garden.

OPPOSITE: Permanent cold frames are placed at the southern facing elevation for protecting tender plants or for establishing plants from seed.

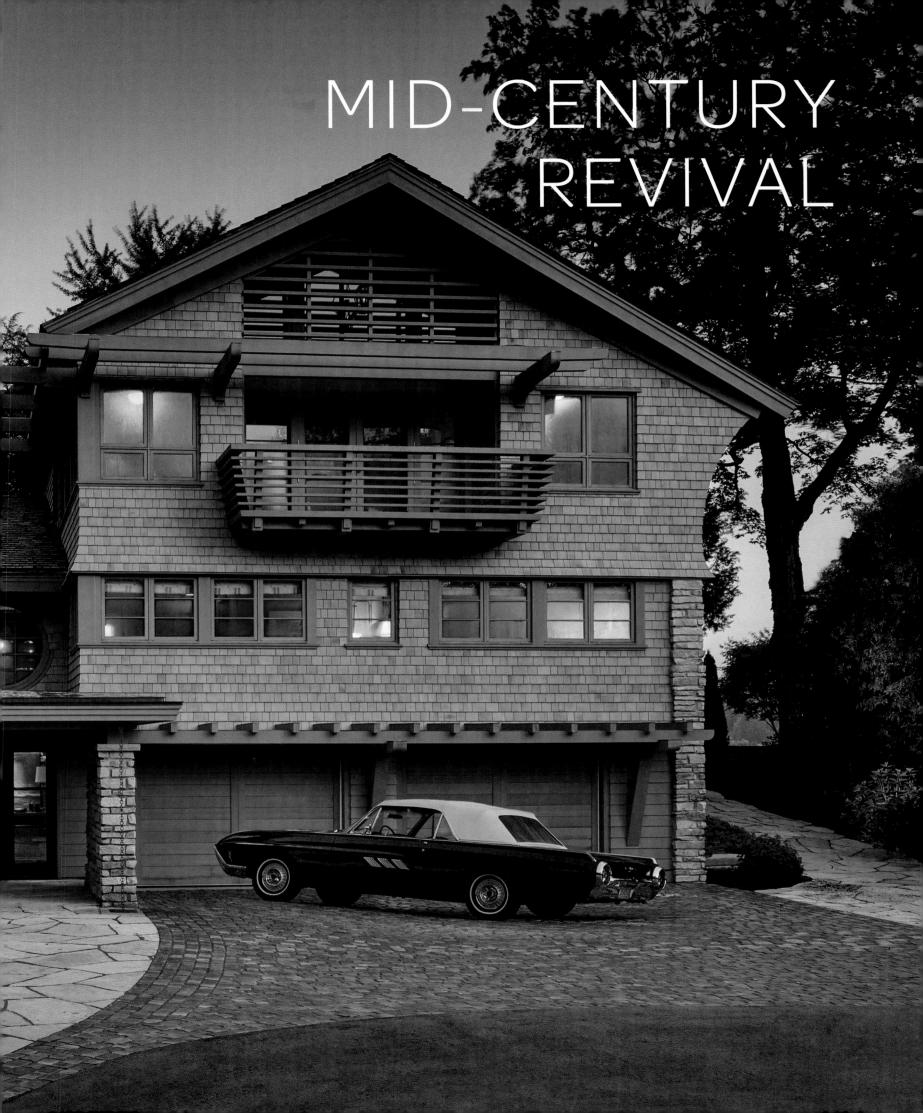

MID-CENTURY
REVIVAL

This lake house had been in our client's family for years and there was a vast history of memories that influenced the conversations about what could be done with the property. He wanted more inside and outside living space and envisioned a modernized version of what was already there. Instead of tearing it down and starting from scratch, we concluded that the house had good bones and unique elements worth keeping. The owner agreed to a gut renovation, which brought the house to a new level for twenty-first century family living and entertaining. Comfort, paired with stylish utility and a nod to nostalgia, guided our designs.

A pleasing composition of wood, stone, and shingle—and the newly added level under a peaked roof—appear at the end of the woodland drive. The balcony above the garage, the casement windows, and a large wood and steel oculus above the entryway are distinct features of the front elevation. A covered walkway along the lower-level leads to the foyer of the house, which opens to a relaxed family game room. Details here and throughout the house have a ship-like sensibility befitting the house's lakeside location.

Midway up the open staircase to the main level, a deep barrel-paneled oculus, built by Heritage Beam and Board and an existing iron wall screen are eye-catching elements. The second floor is a large open space encompassing the kitchen, dining, and living areas with a closed porch that extends the main living space out closer to the water. Up another staircase to the third level of the house is a quiet landing space with options: a perfect spot for curling up to read or pass by on the way to the workout room or the primary suite. Hallways lead to each making the areas very private.

On the main floor, the kitchen takes center stage beneath the generous vaulted ceilings. Our client is a restaurateur and chef, so the main floor revolves around food preparation and gathering people together. A curved banquet nicely defines the breakfast room within the larger space and a mid-century console lends character to a more formal dining area. The geometry of the wall screen inspired many of the details crafted throughout the house. The interiors are the result of a collaborative effort by our team and Peabody's Interiors based in Milwaukee.

Our client was very willing to invest in a significant renovation of a cherished family home, which required both emotional and financial fortitude. Fortuitously, the project was completed just prior to the COVID-19 pandemic, so they were able to enjoy the house, and especially the kitchen, during that time.

PAGES 160–61 AND PRECEDING OVERLEAF
LEFT: A view from the motor court shows the new entry canopy and the incorporation of details such as the full-height wood windows with lattice work for shading. A cantilevered timber deck with horizontal rails demarks the new primary suite level added to the house. The lower ridgeline is original and is over the renovated kitchen space. The exterior features Lannon stone accent walls, flared cedar shingles, and copper gutters.

LEFT AND OVERLEAF: The entryway to the house is on the ground level, which leads to a comfortable family room, sitting area, and bar. The floor grade was lowered to incorporate higher ceilings, and the existing steel stair structure was refreshed. Existing Lannon stone, cerused wood cabinetry with metal inlay, painted shiplap plank, and porcelain tile floors update the space while reinforcing the rustic nature of the home. The sitting area boasts a full-height stone fireplace and access to the lake.

ABOVE: This perspective sketch of main living space and kitchen shows the raised ceiling structure, steel trusses, and cantilevered steel stair that rises to the primary bedroom suite.

OPPOSITE: The main living space looks out through the four-seasons porch to the lake. Bifold doors between the two living areas create more intimate rooms or, when open, a large open space for entertaining. The existing Lannon stone fireplace wall was enlarged in keeping with the increased ceiling height.

OVERLEAF: The new kitchen and butler's pantry are contained within the framework of the existing walls and ceiling. The space has the feeling of being enclosed even while it is integral to the living area's open, light-filled plan. The stainless-steel farmhouse sink, Quartzite countertops, and a custom island of a reclaimed butcher block counter with integrated knife storage are delightful, functional details. A wall of reclaimed barn board and the base of the island are painted in a nautical blue wash. The flooring is white oak random-width plank.

ABOVE: A view from the living space into the kitchen and breakfast buffet. A custom metal hood with steel support appears to hover over the cooking island and reclaimed wood waterfall countertop.

OPPOSITE TOP LEFT: Main cooking island with custom metal hood.

OPPOSITE TOP RIGHT: The breakfast banquette area utilizes an existing decorative metal screen connected to the wall, floor, and ceiling via new steel trusses.

OPPOSITE BOTTOM LEFT: The scullery features open, reclaimed wood shelving (also used in the lower-level family room bar and main living space bar) and a natural stone farmhouse sink. Hand-shaped, ceramic glazed tile is set in a herringbone pattern on the walls.

OPPOSITE BOTTOM RIGHT: Placed comfortably between the

kitchen and living spaces, the dining area is below new exposed steel beams and trusses that support the roof structure.

OVERLEAF LEFT: The primary suite bathroom has a large circular window with a view through trees to the lake. A custom vanity has night lights at the toe kick. Other details include a reclaimed wood beam, the painted tongue-and-groove ceiling, quartz countertop, and Carrara marble flooring tile with an antique finish. The freestanding cast-iron soaking tub is by Waterworks.

OVERLEAF RIGHT: Full-height glazing and a cantilevered deck capture the view from the primary bedroom. Indirect accent lighting is by Anne Kustner Lighting Design.

PAGES 176–77: Above the bar in the main living space, the custom cantilevered steel stair has shaped timber treads and open risers.

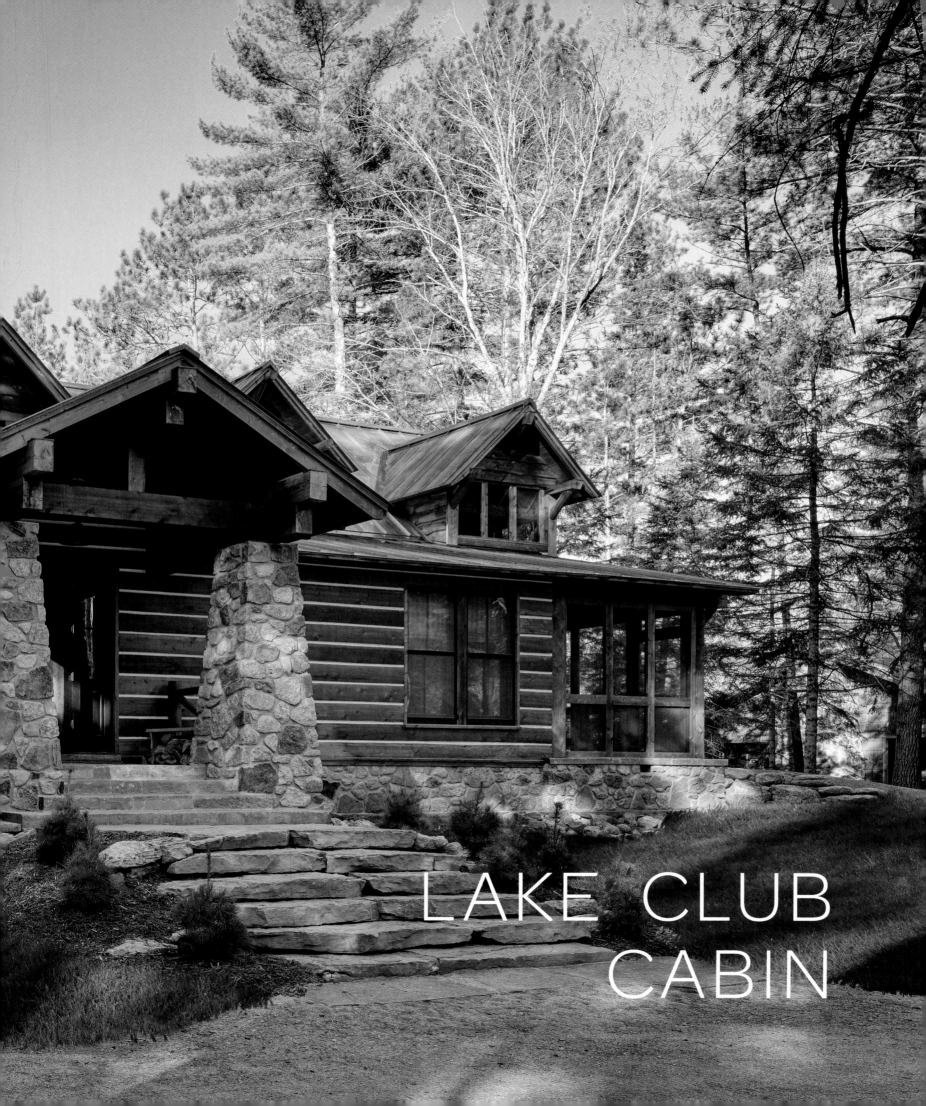

LAKE CLUB
CABIN

In Northern Wisconsin there is a history of lake clubs, enclave-like summertime destinations, that date back a hundred years or more. Often developed by groups of families from Midwestern cities like Milwaukee or Chicago, each club developed distinct camp traditions and strict regulations for use and care of the lakes and waterways. Families owned their mostly rustic cabins and had joint responsibility for the dining hall and management of activities. The long summer days were an immersion in nature and celebration of life.

For this project, the owner's family had a property at one of these fabled lake clubs. She asked us to design a special lodge on par with the original sense of place and its fiercely held traditions, but with more space, amenities, and refinements to make it possible for her family to enjoy it year-round. The summer ritual of places like this, the stuff of time capsules, posed a conundrum: How to expand for future generations without losing the nostalgia that makes it so intriguing in the first place?

The other challenge for this project hinged on the period permitted—mid-September through the winter months to spring—to execute the construction. Key to this push was the local contractor, DeLeers Construction, who respected and understood the complexities and constraints. Engineering and timing were critical. Consultants had restricted access and a long harsh winter made trips arduous during the off-season. The very short summer season likewise made landscaping difficult. Logistically, we had to be acutely aware of the limitations, which perhaps made the project all the more satisfying.

In collaboration with Frank Ponterio, the Chicago- and Naples-based interior designer, we conceived of a two-story lakeside bungalow designed for continuous flow of indoor-outdoor living. The romance of the wooded setting and the mist on the lake are best taken in from the screened-in porches. Timber framing, the stone fireplace, and interior hallway windows for ventilation and light contribute to the character and coziness of the cabin. Conventions like the open-door policy for cocktail hour, communal dining, and summer dances influenced the sensibility while birchbark siding, expansive views, twig furniture, and local stone set the camp ethos. No longer solely a place for the fleeting summer season, the new cabin is ideal for living in nature at any time of year and provides an iconic getaway for generations to come.

PAGES 178–79: The completely handwrought cabin features locally quarried stone, copper standing seam roofing, and bronze screen panels over wooden windows.

PAGE 180: On the lake side, the exterior deck has round timber cross rails and steel cable railing.

PAGES 182–83: The main entry is welcoming with locally made twig and birch benches and hooks on the walls. Overhead is a paneled, pitched birchwood ceiling with wood battens.

OPPOSITE: This view from the entry looks through the main living room—with its dramatic vaulted ceiling—to the screened porch and lake.

LEFT: The realized stair. Custom pine tree cutouts with iron bolt detailing allow light to filter through and add a touch of whimsy.

BELOW: The perspective sketch is a study for the great room space and stair to the guest bedrooms.

RIGHT: The focal point of the house, the great room boasts decorative beams, wood-paneled ceiling, and a generous limestone fireplace. The sliding steel and glass doors lead to the entry; during warmer months, they are left open for the cross breezes from the lake. During winter, they are closed to keep in the warmth from the fire.

OVERLEAF LEFT AND RIGHT: The kitchen is a delightful room with custom cabinetry, vertical beadboard paneling, and open shelving built into a niche in the fireplace. A custom metal hood hangs from chains above the range.

PAGE 190 TOP: Exterior elevation studies.

PAGE 190 BOTTOM: In this moment, the sublime peace and relaxation of this beloved place is captured.

PAGE 191 TOP LEFT: Front entry showing half-log exterior siding and traditional chinking.

PAGE 191 TOP RIGHT: In the ultimate use of local material, a tree trunk found on the property has become a unique chopping block on a hand-forged iron base.

PAGE 191 BOTTOM LEFT AND RIGHT: Details from the sleeping porch include screen panels and the vaulted ceiling. Beds suspended by rope provide the ideal night's sleep.

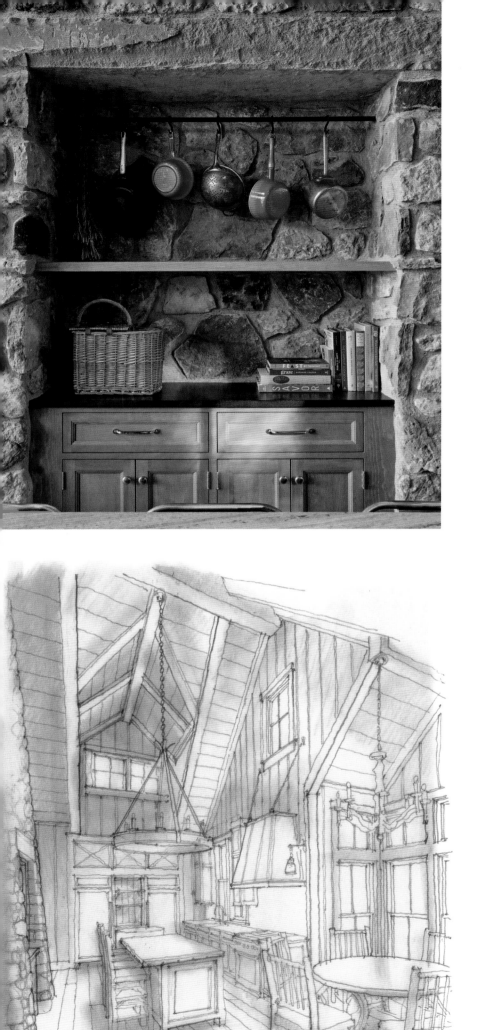

LEFT: The bar/lounge is lined with birch panels for a rustic elegance.

ABOVE: The home office is a pleasant spot with its plaster walls and custom millwork.

OVERLEAF LEFT: The owner's light-filled art studio overlooks the woods at the front of the property.

OVERLEAF RIGHT: Local craftsmen worked with the designer to create this sleeping porch for the younger generation. Bunks are constructed from solid timber, with live-edge siding and side rails of rope threaded through iron eyelets.

PAGE 196 TOP LEFT AND RIGHT: Custom transom "hopper" windows allow the light to flood the otherwise windowless hallway and take advantage of the lake breezes to promote air circulation through the house.

PAGE 196 BOTTOM: Designed for the young visitors, this bunk room features rough-hewn log beds repurposed from the original cabin. Narrow beadboard lines the walls and ceiling for a textured, woodland room.

PAGE 197: Floor-to-ceiling windows offer this cozy guest bedroom a spectacular view of the lake.

ABOVE: Tucked into a second-floor dormer, the guest bath is flooded with natural light. A green enameled tub rests on a hexagonal tile floor. Vintage plumbing and light fixtures reminiscent of the original cabin offer historical character to the space.

OPPOSITE: A second-floor bedroom is like a treehouse sanctuary. Birch panels and dogwood branches line the walls and cover built-in closets to maintain the serene simplicity. An iron and parchment ceiling fixture and natural textiles contribute to the camp-like sensibility evident throughout the house.

OVERLEAF: The screened porch design integrates a mix of natural and local materials that achieve the goal of making the house feel handcrafted and authentic to the place. Inside and out, the house and its lakeside property are a special retreat for all ages.

PAGES 202–03: This lakeside elevation shows off the textures of the house that completely succeed in capturing the nostalgia for the old cabin and revered lake club traditions while offering the clients' extended family modernized, year-round enjoyment and respite.

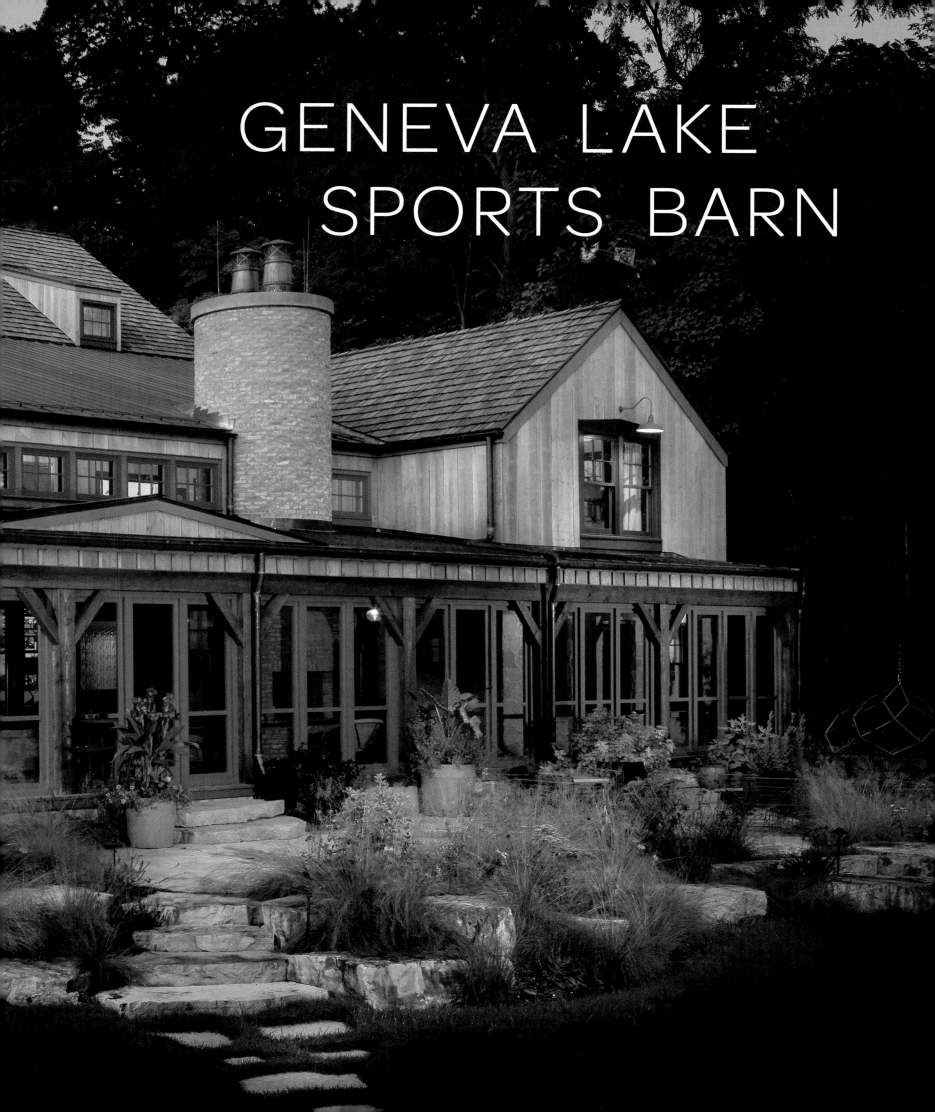

GENEVA LAKE
SPORTS BARN

A decade or so ago our clients engaged us to design a rambling, shingle-style weekend house. When they were eventually able to purchase the property adjacent to that house, they called upon us once again as they began to imagine an athletic facility that sparked their imaginations and inspired ours as well. They envisioned a multiuse structure that would complete their getaway compound and offer a wide range of amenities for family and friends. The idea of a barn adapted to house all the activities was the narrative goal from the beginning. The fun for us all came from imagining what an old barn would look like, how it would have been sited in the landscape a hundred years ago, and how a new old barn could be made useful and contemporary in this context.

Among the many iterations to accommodate the extremely complex program, some of our earliest sketches were remarkably close to what the realized structure became. The owners requested appropriately designed spaces for a variety of athletic pursuits: volleyball, basketball, tennis, and water sports, to name a few. They also wanted an entertainment area, game room, bunk rooms upstairs for kid sleepovers, an office, and a big screened-in porch. Locker rooms, a spa, kitchen, and a silo-like brick fireplace are additional features.

In the process of working with the challenging terrain, which included a previously built man-made pond, it became important to the client to restore the indigenous landscape. We worked closely with landscape and water engineering experts to integrate the two properties as one, remove invasive species, create a new pool, rebuild old retaining walls, and restore the wetlands. In the winter, heavy rains are diverted to flood a low, flat area between the barn and the lake. When it freezes, it becomes a hockey rink, and we designed a warming house that sits at the ready nearby.

While the entirety of the commission required highly technical design, the rustic agrarian forms and reclaimed materials employed give a sense of history to this newly built structure. The warmth and playfulness of the outcome—and the extreme utility—successfully reflects the intentions, vision, and imagination brought forth when a team works with purpose and cohesion to turn a dream into a reality.

ABOVE AND OPPOSITE: An L-shaped screened-in porch wraps around from one side to span the entire length of the rear elevation.

OVERLEAF TOP LEFT: Within the porch, the silo bisects the space with a silhouette fireplace of Chicago Brick. Aged copper hanging lanterns from Remains Lighting line the ceiling from antiqued hooks and the stenciled floor is by Roux.

OVERLEAF RIGHT: Inside, the silo provides another fireplace adjacent to the refurbished stair by Alpine Woodworking.

OPPOSITE AND ABOVE: Across from the stair, the large open living area invites with an assemblage of antique accessories and furnishings that include an oak parlor bar purchased from Salvage One in Chicago. Reclaimed barnwood flooring and board and batten walls lend a warm age to the interior, while the over-the-top crystal chandeliers from Big Daddy's Antiques add unexpected glamour.

ABOVE AND RIGHT: The basketball court on the other side of the living area is accessible via sliding barn doors inset with antique cast iron grill panels. The extraordinary 16-foot-tall glass and iron screen, created for the Chicago Red Cross building, depicts scenes of workers. Restored and installed into the wall dividing the gym from the living room, it makes an artistic and historic statement in this context.

OVERLEAF LEFT AND RIGHT: The loft above is filled with vintage arcade games and an operable phone booth. A line of Moravian star lanterns float above the shuffleboard table.

ABOVE: A reclaimed, carved-stone, pasture drinking vessel has been refashioned into a statement sink. It is flanked by dramatic iron sconces that have been stripped of layers of paint to reveal their original charm. Bath tile is by Daltile.

OPPOSITE: A bird's-eye view of the lake and an interior woodland scheme are punctuated with playful pops of color. A modern chandelier and industrial bunk beds complete this cheery space.

LAKESIDE
ESCAPE

For repeat clients with a very long personal relationship—having known both since grade school—our firm was delighted to help conceive and design a multigenerational lakeside retreat. Knowing the family well offered us a unique perspective on the owners' desire to extend a family legacy already in place. Decades ago, the husband's great-grandfather established a lakeside vacation retreat, but as the family grew, it became a scheduling challenge for everyone to use the beloved house. Remarkably, three contiguous properties directly across the lake became available and the owners envisioned a new destination to accommodate their kids and grandchildren while continuing the tradition of summers at the lake and year-round enjoyment.

The new properties, each with extant seasonal cottages, fronted a private road. The clients imagined building two new residences to replace the cottages. Not a main house and a guesthouse, but rather two fully independent yet complementary structures with designated suites for families and bunk rooms for the kids and their friends. Two boathouses and other outbuildings made up the existing structures. On the lake side, directly opposite the boathouses, was a clear view of the great-grandfather's property that had been the scene of countless family gatherings.

As we set to work on creating a new family destination, the pieces began to fall into place. Two residences were designed to fit on the combined, yet narrow lots. Both boathouses were re-envisioned, one more rustic and the other, once permitted by the county, became a party pavilion on the lake where all the kids love to hang out.

The first house, known as the South House, was completed by Thanksgiving 2019 and the family intended to live in it during construction of the North House, which was delayed during the COVID-19 pandemic. Fortunately, the completed South House became the ideal refuge for the extended family during that uncertain time.

The clients were extremely attentive to the design details throughout the construction process. They wanted details to be architecturally correct and were sensitive to how a pair of side-by-side, substantial homes would appear from the water. To minimize the massing, we brought down the eave lines to the second story and visually created the impression of a charming collection of smaller buildings rather than two large homes. The North House features a media room, hot tub, and spa on the lake side and, to reduce the visual impact, an open-air grotto for these amenities was recessed into the land, creating a respite space protected from the winds.

The western siting of the houses and the interior plans likewise intentionally offer moments of surprise, whether framing the astonishing sunsets and the choice of water views upon entering, or the spaces that belie the largeness of the home. We rendered the scale of the rooms to be welcoming and intimate, such as the outdoor porch or the upstairs bedrooms that are sized to give the impression that previous service quarters were converted for use by family and friends. Reduced ceilings, dormer windows, and framed-out spaces in these rooms are captivating and draw people in like an embrace.

It's important to note that our clients set the tone from the beginning: they were firmly dedicated to the creation of a new heirloom property and made lasting choices. They insisted on quality materials, desiring the functional utility to be at the same high level as their aesthetic demand. Our design team, our contractor, many craftsmen, Scott Byron & Co. for landscape design, and Teresa Manns Design all helped fulfill the dream. It was an exciting opportunity for all of us at WWA to make the details, down to the trim and paint choices, absolutely right. The new structures on the property are so appropriate to the place that they are frequently mistaken for an old family vacation compound that has been renovated. Thus, a quintessential lakeside tradition is preserved, enhanced, and will continue for generations.

PRECEDING OVERLEAF RIGHT: The south entry of the South House presents a classically inspired, yet informal design. The locally sourced fieldstone veneer is a warm backdrop for the dark gray operable shutters and the slate of the gambrel roof. Rural vernacular farmhouse roofs inspired the design.

OPPOSITE: A massive fieldstone chimney with zinc-coated copper flashing and clay chimney pots with antique glaze is a dominant feature of the North House. An oriel bay window overlooks the lawn between the North and South houses. Lightning rods with glass strike indicator balls give the impression the house is from an earlier time.

ABOVE AND RIGHT: The South House living room is graced with deep elliptical jambs that frame the view to the stair hall and large kitchen. The stair design was inspired by a house in Newport, Rhode Island. Wide plank floors lend a note of age and character to the room.

OVERLEAF LEFT: A vintage mantel adds a note of gravitas against the shiplap paneling.

OVERLEAF RIGHT: Double-hung windows with lug details frame the natural beauty of the site.

The South House kitchen opens broadly to the dining area; both spaces are designed to accommodate large gatherings. Nautically inspired pendant fixtures illuminate the space above the large island countertop and breakfast bar. Full overlay panels integrate fixtures into the cabinetry.

OPPOSITE: The apothecary drawers on the vast kitchen island help minimize its large scale. The stove hood has metal strap detail and an enamel finish.

ABOVE: The adjacent butler's pantry is fully functional with refrigerator, service bar, custom-built cabinets, and stained-wood countertop.

OVERLEAF LEFT AND RIGHT: The lower-level, ship-shape bunk room in the South House is neatly designed with mahogany ship's

ladders and storage below. For the bath, two full water closets with sliding barn doors flank the custom concrete sink.

PAGES 238: The gambrel roof shape provides a generous interior hall that leads to the bedrooms. At the end of the hall is a lovely, light-filled sitting area.

PAGE 239: The garage roof shape and dormers render a charming guest suite kitchenette.

The North House is substantial with complex fenestration and a classically detailed entry. Shed dormers and shingle siding over shiplap define the exterior along with stone veneer. A gable roof with Greek returns frame the primary balcony over the living room bay. Bifold shutters afford asymmetrical protection, and the windows have integrated flower boxes.

OVERLEAF TOP LEFT AND RIGHT: Interior and exterior of the guest suite cupola.

OVERLEAF BOTTOM LEFT AND RIGHT: Grotto spa and exterior detail of horizontal shiplap siding.

OVERLEAF RIGHT: Pediment with finial above the breezeway door. The cedar shingle has three coats of transparent "evergreen" stain.

PRECEDING OVERLEAF, ABOVE, AND OPPOSITE BOTTOM: The expansive first floor of the North House flows from the entry to the comfortable dining and living rooms.

OPPOSITE TOP: The mirror above the wood-burning fireplace disguises a large television.

ABOVE AND RIGHT: The inviting study in the North House has waxed-aged pine paneling.

OVERLEAF LEFT AND RIGHT: The kitchen features a paneled and pitched ceiling, cove lighting, and inset cabinetry with a farmhouse sink. A banquette contributes to a cozy breakfast corner.

OPPOSITE: The North House stair has painted spindles and stained mahogany treads, newel posts, and railing.

ABOVE: En route to the bedrooms, the ceiling of the upper-level foyer has a gleaming lacquered finish to reflect the light in this windowless space.

OVERLEAF: Captivating views, heated herringbone brick flooring, and a fireplace of local fieldstone make the South House screened porch a year-round gathering space.

PAGE 256: The walk-though butler's pantry in the North House has a handy integrated ladder and illuminated white oak cabinetry.

PAGE 257: The sheen of vintage Chris Craft boats influenced the design of this high-gloss mahogany bar.

OPPOSITE AND ABOVE: The renovated North boathouse nestles neatly into the surrounding landscape. The upper level boasts panoramic lake views, providing abundant seating options, including built-in bench seating, to accommodate friends and family. An integrated, hidden lift television cabinet provides entertainment options for rainy days.

ABOVE AND OPPOSITE: The South boathouse was remodeled to include a large viewing deck cantilevered over the water by large brackets. Fieldstone veneer and carriage-style doors for boat access make the structure picturesque and functional.

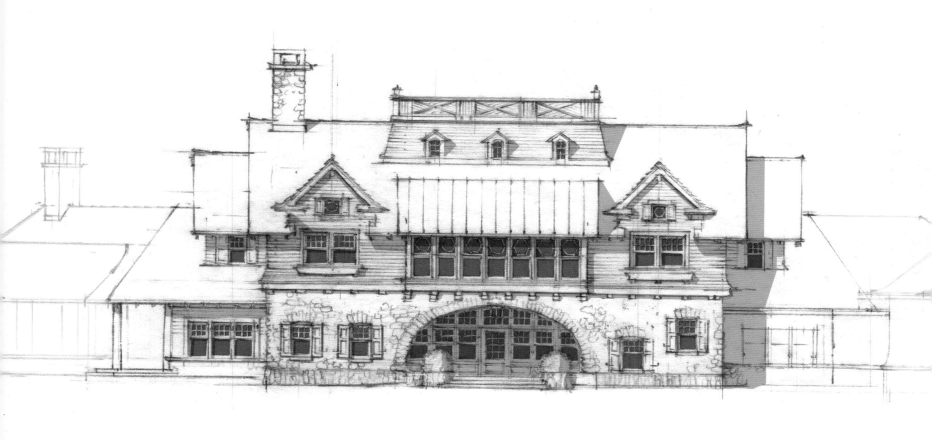

DRAWING
INSPIRATION

CREDITS

FRONT MATTER

Photos:
  © 2024 Dustin Halleck–2, 4
  © 2024 Rocco Ceselin–7

CALIFORNIA FARM RETREAT

Photos:
  © 2024 Wade Weissmann Architecture–12(T) © 2024 Doug Edmunds–14(B), 17, 18, 32–33 © 2024 Holly LePere–8–9,. 12–13(R), 14(T), 16(L), 15, 16–17, 19–32

Architect of Record–Stuart Magruder, Studio Nova A

General Contractor–All Coast Construction

Landscape Design–Arcadia Studio

Interior Design–Simonds Design, Jorje Design, Studio Beppa, Ltd.

NEW STRUCTURES FOR A STORIED ESTATE

Photos:
  © 2024 David Bader34–43
  © 2024 Dustin Halleck–44–49

General Contractor–Treg's Woodwork & Constrction

Landscape Design–LandWorks

Interior Design–Candyce Tice of Wade Weissmann Architecture

BAY VILLA

Photographic Credits:
  © 2024 Karyn Millet–50–55, 57R, 58–60, 62–75, 77
  ©2024 Michael Stavaridis–56, 61, 76, 78–79

General Contractor–Brodson Construction

Landscape Design–Page Duke and CLAD Landscape

Interior Design–Mark Weaver & Associates

LAKE MICHIGAN MODERN

Photos:
  © 2024 Dustin Halleck–80–93

General Contractor–Moore Designs, Inc.

Landscape Design–LandWorks

Interior Design–Karen Kempf Interiors

PEACEFIELD FARM

Photos:
  © 2024 Caroline Allison–94–113

General Contractor–Davis Properties

Interior Design–Rachel Halvorson Designs

GEORGIAN COUNTRY ESTATE

Photos:
  © 2024 Francesco Lagnese–124–131, 132–45, 148
  © 2024 Eric Piasecki–114–23, 146–47

General Contractor–Crapsey & Gilles

Landscape Design–Page Landscape

Interior Design–Williams Lawrence

MIDWEST GREENHOUSE

Photos:
  © 2024 Dustin Halleck–150–59

General Contractor–Jorndt Fahey, LLC

Landscape Design–Scott Byron & Co., Inc.

Interior Design–Candyce Tice of Wade Weissmann Architecture

MID-CENTURY REVIVAL

Photos:
  © 2024 Dustin Halleck–160–77

General Contractor–Burg Homes, LLC

Landscape Design–LandWorks

Interior Design–Jennifer Schuppie for Peabody's Interiors and Candyce Tyce of Wade Weissmann Architecture

LAKE CLUB CABIN

Photos:
  © 2024 Dustin Halleck–178–203

General Contractor–DeLeers Construction

Interior Design–Frank Ponterio

GENEVA LAKE SPORTS BARN

Photos:
  © 2024 David Bader–204–19

General Contractor–Harold O. Schultz

Landscape Design–Kane Brothers

Interior Design–Simonds Design, Studio Beppa, Ltd.

LAKESIDE ESCAPE

Photos:
  © 2024 Dustin Halleck–220–61

General Contractor–Colby Construction

Landscape Design–Scott Byron & Co., Inc.

Interior Design–Teresa Manns Design

First edition
28 27 26 25 24   5 4 3 2 1
Text © 2024 by Wade Weissmann Architecture
Illustrations © 2024 by Wade Weissmann Architecture
Photographic credits above

All rights reserved. No part of this book may be reproduced by any means whatsoever without written permission from the publisher, except brief portions quoted for purpose of review.

Published by
Gibbs Smith
570 North Sportsplex Dr
Kaysville, Utah 84037
1.800.835.4993 orders
www.gibbs-smith.com

Designed by Virginia Brimhall Snow
Printed and bound in China

Library of Congress Control Number: 2024930622
ISBN: 978-1-4236-6506-9

This product is made of FSC®-certified and other controlled materials.

MIX
Paper | Supporting responsible forestry
FSC® C153458